Hacking University:
Freshman Edition

Essential Beginner's Guide on How to Become an Amateur Hacker (Hacking, How to Hack, Hacking for Beginners, Computer Hacking)

By Isaac D. Cody

HACKING UNIVERSITY

FRESHMAN EDITION

Essential Beginner's Guide on How to Become an Amateur Hacker
(Hacking, How to Hack, Hacking for Beginners, Computer Hacking)

ISAAC D. CODY

Table of Contents

Preview

Do you ever wonder what the future holds in terms of computer security and computer hacking? Have you ever wondered if hacking is right for you?

It is estimated that a Certified Ethical Hacker earns on average $71,000. Differentiate yourself and learn what it means to become a hacker!

This book will provide you the ultimate guide in how to actually start and begin how to learn Computer Hacking. I firmly believe with the right motivation, ethics, and passion, *anyone* can be a hacker.

"Hacking University: Freshman Edition. Essential Beginner's Guide on How to Become an Amateur Hacker will encompass a wide array of topics that will <u>lay the foundation of computer hacking AND *actually* enable you to start hacking.</u>

Some of the topics covered in this book include:

- **The History of Hacking**

- **Benefits and Dangers of Hacking**

- **The Future of Cybersecurity**

- **Essential Basics to Start Hacking**

- **Computer Networks**

- **Hacking in terms of Hardware and Software**

- **Penetration Testing**

- **Cracking Passwords**

- **Backdoors**

- **Trojans**

- **Information Security**

- **Network Scan and VPN**

- **Viruses**

Believe it or not there are just a few of the topics covered in this book. "Hacking University: Freshman Edition. Essential Beginner's Guide on How to Become an Amateur Hacker (Hacking, How to Hack, Hacking for Beginners, Computer Hacking) will cover much more related topics to this.

Introduction

I want to thank you and congratulate you for downloading the book Hacking University: Freshman Edition. This book is the definitive starters guide for information on hacking. Whether you are a security professional or an aspiring hacktivist, this book provides you with definitions, resources, and demonstrations for the novice.

Hacking is a divisive subject, but it is a matter of fact that hacking is used for benevolent purposes as well as malevolent. Hacking is needed, for otherwise how would incompetence and abuse be brought to light? Equally, the "Hacker's Manifesto" explains the ideology of hackers- they are guilty of no crime, save curiosity. Experimenting with systems is inherently fun, and it offers exceptionally gifted people an outlet for their inquisitiveness. This book continues those ethics; the demonstrations made available here are written in good faith for the sake of education and enjoyment.

Nonetheless federal governments hack each other to steal classified information, groups hack corporations on a political agenda, and individuals exploit other people for revenge. These examples do not represent hackers, and the aforementioned scenarios are not what good-natured, curious hackers would do. This book does not condone these types of hacks either.

As a disclaimer, though- nobody is responsible for any damage caused except for yourself. Some demonstrations in this book are potentially dangerous, so by performing them you are doing so willingly of your own accord and with explicit permission from the computer and network owners.

And for the non-hackers reading, there's an inescapable fact- you will need the information in this book to protect yourself. You will learn what hackers look for and how they exploit security weaknesses. Therefore, you will be able to protect yourself more fully from their threats. Lastly, if you do not develop your knowledge in this field, you will inevitably fall behind. Complacency leads to vulnerability in the computer world, so this book could be the one that clues you in on just how important security and hacking are.

It's time for you to become an amazing hacker. Studying the history of the art form will give you an appreciation and background, so we will begin there. Read on and begin your career of security.

Chapter 1: History and Famous Hacks

Hacking has a rich a varied history beginning far back in ancient times. Cryptography and encryption (passwords) were used by Roman armies. A commander would need to send orders across the battlefield and would do so by writing instructions on a piece of paper. Foot-soldiers could run the papers back and forth and thus one side would gain an advantage with increased knowledge.

Undoubtedly the soldiers would sometimes be captured and the secret orders would fall into the wrong hands. To combat this, commanders began obscuring the text by transforming and moving around the letters. This process, known as encryption, succeeded in confusing enemy commanders until they were forced to attempt to break the encryption. Employing mathematical methods and clever tricks to un-obfuscate the orders, the enemy would sometimes be able to decode the text. Therefore, ancient people were hacking long before computers were even conceived!

However, when most people imagine early hacking, they are usually drawn to the wildly interesting story of the Enigma Machine. The Enigma machine was a device used famously in Nazi Germany during the 2nd World War to encrypt and decrypt war messages. Much like the ancient Romans, the German messages were obfuscated and transformed before sending so that if the message might be intercepted, the opposition would be unable to read the highly secretive text. Besides a brief moment in the 1930's where the encryption method was discovered, the Enigma machine was very successful for much of its existence. Polish cryptologists were the ones to initially break the code, but Germany countered later in the decade by improving on the design and making Enigma far more complicated.

The rein of Enigma continued throughout the war. An American professor by the name of Alan Turing used his studies and extensive knowledge of mathematics to provide key research that broke the Enigma code again in 1939. As it usually is with encryption methods though, Enigma was improved again and made unbreakable until 1943 when Turing assisted the Navy and produced a faster decryption machine.

"Bombes", as they were called, were the decryption machines the facilitated cracking the Enigma code. Bombe machines used rotating drums and electrical signals to analyze the scrambled messages and output the correct configuration of dials and plugs that would result in a decoded text. Bombes could almost be considered some of the earliest computers due to their mechanical and electrical complexity. Despite the highly advanced technology put forth from both sides, Enigma's final demise actually came about from the allied capture of the secret keys, or codes, used in the machine. With the encryption method clear, Enigma became mostly useless baring another redesign. A redesign couldn't come soon enough, as the war soon ended. The allied ability to decode Enigma messages definitely played a large part in their success.

After World War II, an immense amount of research and calculations went into developing projectile missiles and nuclear weapons. The Cold War essentially facilitated the development of modern electrical computers because electronic devices could perform mathematics at a speedy pace. Advanced devices such as Colossus, ENIAC, and EDSAC paved the way for faster electronics throughout the 1950s and 1960s. Supercomputers were used in universities and corporations around the world, and these early devices were susceptible to intrusion and hacking as well. However, the most notable 20th century hacking movement was known as Phreaking, and it involved "hacking" through telephones.

Phreaking began after phone companies switched from human operators to automated switches. Automated switches determined where to route a phone call based on the tonal frequency generated by telephones when numbers were dialed. The pitched beeps heard when pressing buttons on cell phones is reminiscent of this, as each button produces a differently pitched tone. Tones in succession dialed numbers with automatic switches, and the phone user would have their call connected to the number dialed.

Certain other tones translated to different actions, though- phreakers discovered that by imitating the special tones they could control the automated switches and get free long-distance phone calls across the world. Phreaking then evolved into a culture of individuals who would explore and experiment with phone systems, often delving into illegal methods to have fun and evade fees. Skilled phreakers could even eavesdrop on phone calls and manipulate phone company employees by impersonating technical staff.

A few phreakers became famous within the community for discovering new techniques and furthering the phreaking study. Joseph Engressia was the first to discover the tone needed to make long distance calls, and John "Captain Crunch" Draper found that a prize whistle within a cereal box produced that exact tone, and he gained his nickname from that finding. Interviews of prominent phreakers inspired later generations- Steve Jobs himself liked to partake in the hobby.

Networked computers and the invention of BBS brought the culture to even more people, so the pastime grew tremendously. No longer a small movement, the government took notice in 1990 when phreaking communities were targeted by the United States Secret Service through Operation Sundevil. The operation saw a few phreaking groups shut down for illegal activity. As time progressed, landlines became increasingly less popular having to compete with cell phones, so phreaking mostly died in the 1990s. Mostly, phreaking culture sidestepped and got absorbed into hacking culture when personal computers became affordable to most families.

By the mid-1980s, corporations and government facilities were being hacked into regularly by hobbyists and "white-hat" professionals who report computer vulnerabilities. Loyd Blankenship wrote the "Hacker Manifesto" on an online magazine viewed by hackers and phreakers in 1986; the document later became a key piece in the philosophy of hackers as it attributes them as curious individuals who are not guilty of crime. Hacking continued to develop and in 1988 Robert Morris created a computer worm that crashed Cornell University's computer system. Although likely not malicious, this situation marked a division in computer hacking. Some individuals continued to have fun as "white-hats" and others sought illegal personal gain as "black-hat" hackers.

The most popular hacker group today is most definitely Anonymous. The aptly-named group is essentially hidden and member-less because it performs "operations" that any person can join, usually by voluntarily joining a botnet and DDoSing (these terms will be discussed further in subsequent chapters). Anonymous is most popular for their "raids" on Habbo Hotel, scientology, and Paypal. While some actions the group take seem contradictory to past action or counter-intuitive, these facts make sense because Anonymous does not have a defined membership and actions are taken by individuals claiming to be part of the group- there are no core members. Many news outlets label Anonymous as a terrorist group, and constant hacking operations keep the group in the public eye today.

Edward Snowden became a household name in 2013 when he leaked sensitive documents from the National Security Agency that revealed the US government's domestic and worldwide surveillance programs. Snowden is hailed as a hero by those that believe the surveillance was unwarranted, obtrusive, and an invasion of privacy. Opponents of Snowden claim he is a terrorist who leaked private data of the government. No matter which way the situation is viewed, it becomes clear that hacking and cybersecurity are grand-scale issues in the modern world.

Having always-connected internet has exposed almost every computer as vulnerable. Cybersecurity is now a major concern for every government, corporation, and individual. Hacking is a necessary entity in the modern world, no matter if it is used for "good" or "evil". As computers are so prevalent and interweaved with typical function, hackers will be needed constantly for professional security positions. It is only through studying the past, though, that we can learn about the unique situation that modern hacking is in.

Chapter 2: Modern Security

IT professionals today usually do not fill "jack-of-all-trades" positions in corporations. While a small business may still employ a single person who is moderately proficient in most areas of technology, the huge demands imposed on internet connected big businesses means that several IT specialists must be present concurrently. Low-level help-desk personnel report to IT managers who report to administrators who report to the CTO (Chief Technology Officer). Additionally, sometimes there are even further specializations where security employees confer with administrators and report to a CIO (Chief Information Officer) or CSO (Chief Security Officer). Overall, security must be present in companies either full-time, contracted through a 3rd party, or through dual specialization of a system administrator. Annually a large amount of revenue is lost due to data breaches, cyber-theft, DDOS attacks, and ransomware. Hackers perpetuate the constant need for security while anti-hackers play catch-up to protect assets.

The role of a security professional is to confirm to the best of their ability the integrity of all the security of an organization. Below are a few explanations of the various areas of study that security professionals protect from threats. Some of these "domains" are also the key areas of study for CISSP

(Certified Information System Security Professional) certificate holders, which is a proof of proficiency in security. CISSPs are sometimes considered anti-hackers because they employ their knowledge to stop hackers before the problem can even occur.

Network Security

Network security includes protecting a networked server from outside intrusion. This means that there cannot be any entry point for curious individuals to gain access. Data sent through the network should not be able to be intercepted or read, and sometimes encryption is needed to ensure compromised data is not useful to a hacker.

Access Control

A sophisticated security infrastructure needs to be able to identify and authenticate authorized individuals. Security professionals use methods such as passwords, biometrics, and two-factor authentication to make sure that a computer user really is who they say they are. Hackers attempt to disguise themselves as another user by stealing their password or finding loopholes.

Software Application Security

Hackers are quick to exploit hidden bugs and loopholes in software that could elevate their privilege and give them access to secret data. Since most corporations and governments run their own in-house proprietary software, security professionals cannot always fully test software for problems. This is a popular areas for hackers to exploit, because bugs and loopholes are potentially numerous.

Disaster Recovery

Sometimes the hacker is successful. A skilled troublemaker can infiltrate remote servers and deal great damage or steal a plethora of information; disaster recovery is how security professionals respond. Often, there are documents that have a specific plan for most common disaster situations. Automated recognition systems can tell when an intrusion has occurred or when data has been stolen, and the best CISSPs can shut down the hack or even reverse-track the culprit to reveal their true identity. Disaster recovery is not always a response to attacks, though. Natural disasters count too, and there is nothing worse than a flooded server room. Professionals must have a disaster plan to get their business back up and running or else the business could face a substantial loss of money.

Encryption and Cryptography

As we've learned by looking at history, the encryption of data is a valuable tool that can protect the most valuable information. For every encryption method, though, there is a hacker/cracker using their talents to break it. Security personnel use cryptography to encrypt sensitive files, and hackers break that encryption. Competent hackers can break weak encryption by having a strong computer (that can perform fast math), or by finding flaws in the encryption algorithms.

Risk Management

Is it worth it? Every addition to computer infrastructure comes with a risk. Networked printers are extremely helpful to businesses, but hackers have a reputation for gaining access to a network by exploiting vulnerabilities in the printer software. When anything is going to be changed, IT staff must weigh the risk versus the benefit to conclude whether change is a safe idea. After all, adding that Wi-Fi-enabled coffee pot may just give a hacker the entry point they need.

Physical Security

A common theme in cyberpunk novels (a literary subgenre about hackers) involves breaking into a building at night and compromising the network from within. This is a real threat, because any person that has physical access to a computer has a significant advantage when it comes to hacking. Physical security involves restricting actual bodily access to parts of a building or locking doors so a hacker doesn't have the chance to slip by and walk off with an HDD.

Operations

Many, many notable hacks were performed by employees of the organization that had too many access permissions. Using the information and access that they are granted, these hackers commit an "inside job" and make off with their goals. Security teams attempt to prevent this by only giving just enough access to everyone that they need to do their job. It just goes to show, security staff cannot even trust their coworkers.

These are not all of the CISSP domains, but they are the most notable. Interestingly, the domains give an insight into the methodology and philosophy that security IT have when protecting data, and how hackers have to be wary of exactly how CISSPs operate.

The most useful knowledge about modern security for hackers, though, is an intimate idea of how businesses conduct operations. Understanding that most businesses store data on a server and authenticate themselves through Windows domains is a decent first step, but real-world experience is needed to actually understand what makes computer infrastructure tick.

Chapter 3: Common Terms

One important aspect of hacking involves a deep understanding of a multitude of computing concepts. In this chapter, we will broadly cover a few important ones.

Programming

The skill of writing instructional code for a computer is known as programming. Original programming was done with only binary 1s and 0s. Programming nowadays is done with high-level programming languages that are decently close to plain English with special characters mixed in. Programs must be compiled, which means translated into machine code before they can run. Understanding the basics of programming gives a hacker much insight into how the applications they are trying to exploit work, which might just give them an edge.

Algorithms

Algorithms are repeated tasks that lead to a result. For example, multiplication problems can be solved through an algorithm that repeatedly adds numbers. 5 x 3 is the same as 5 + 5 + 5. Algorithms are the basis of encryption- repeated scrambling is done to data to obfuscate it.

Cryptography

Cryptography is the study and practice of encryption and decryption. Encrypting a file involves scrambling the data contents around through a variety of algorithms. The more complex the algorithm, the harder the encryption is to reverse, or decrypt. Important files are almost always encrypted so they cannot be read without the password that begins the decryption. Encryption can be undone through various other means, too, such as cryptoanalysis (intense evaluation and study of data patterns that might lead to discovering the password) or attacks.

Passwords

Passwords are a key phrases that authenticates a user to access information not usually accessible to those not authorized. We use passwords for just about everything in computers, and cracking passwords is a prize for most hackers. Passwords can be compromised many different ways, but mostly through database leaks, social engineering, or weak passwords.

Hardware

The physical components of a computer that make them work. Here's a small security tidbit: the US government is sometimes worried that hardware coming from China is engineered in such a way that would allow China to hack into US government computers.

Software

Software is any program of written code that performs a task. Software examples range from word processors to web browsers to operating systems. Software can also be referred to as programs, applications, and apps.

Scripts

A small piece of code that achieves a simple task can be called a script. Usually not a full-fledged program or software because it is just too small.

Operating Systems

The large piece of software on a computer that is used as a framework for other smaller applications is called an operating system or OS. Most computers run a variant of Microsoft operating systems, but some use Apple OSX or GNU+Linux-based operating systems.

Linux

Simply put, Linux is a kernel (kernel = underlying OS code) that facilitates complex operating systems. While Windows uses the NT kernel as a core, operating systems such as Ubuntu and Debian use the Linux kernel as a core. Linux operating systems are very different from the ones we are used to, because they do not run .exe files or have a familiar interface. In fact, some Linux operating systems are purely text-based. Linux, though, is very powerful to a hacker because it can run software that Windows cannot, and some of this software is designed with security and hacking specifically in mind. We will see in later chapters how Linux can be used to our advantage.

Computer Viruses

A broad term that usually encompasses a variety of threats. It can mean virus, worm, Trojan, malware, or any other malicious piece of software. Specifically, a virus in particular is a self-replicating harmful program. Viruses copy themselves to other computers and continue to infect like the common cold. Some viruses are meant to annoy the user, others are meant to destroy a system, and some even hide and cause unseen damage behind the scenes.

Strange computer activity or general slowness can sometimes be a virus.

Worms

Worms are malicious pieces of code that do not need a host computer. Worms "crawl" through networks and have far reaching infections.

Trojans

Named from the ancient "Trojan Horse", Trojans are bad software that are disguised as helpful programs. If you've ever got an infection from downloading a program on the internet, then you were hit by a Trojan. Trojans are often bundled in software installations and copied alongside actually helpful programs.

Malware

Malware is a general and generic term for mischievous programs, such as scripts, ransomware, and all those mentioned above.

Ransomware

Ransomware is a specific type of malware that cleverly encrypts user's files and demands payment for the decryption password. Highly effective, as large businesses that require their data be always available (hospitals, schools, etc...) usually have to pay the fee to continue business.

Botnet

Worms and other types of malware sometimes infect computers with a larger purpose. Botnets are interconnected networks of infected computers that respond to a hacker's bidding. Infected "zombies" can be made to run as a group and pool resources for massive DDoS attacks that shut down corporate and government websites. Some botnet groups use the massive combined computing power to brute-force passwords and decrypt data. Being part of a malicious botnet is never beneficial.

Proxy

There exist helpful tools for hackers and individuals concerned with privacy. Proxies are services that route your internet content to another place as to hide your true location. For example, if you were to post online though a proxy located in Sweden, the post would look as though it was initially created in Sweden, rather than where you actually live. Hackers use proxies to hide their true location should they ever be found out. Security-concerned people use proxies to throw off obtrusive surveillance.

VPN

A Virtual Private Network is a service/program that "tunnels" internet traffic. It works very much like a proxy, but can hide various other information in addition to encryption of the internet packets. VPNs are typically used by business employees that work away from the office. An employee can connect to their VPN and they will be tunneled through to the corporate server and can access data as if they were sitting in an office work chair. VPNs can be used by hackers to hide location and data information, or to create a direct link to their target. A VPN link to an office server will certainly give more privilege than an average internet connection would.

Penetration Testing

Penetration testing, or pen testing, is the benevolent act of searching for vulnerabilities in security that a hacker might use to their advantage. Security experts can do pen testing as a full time job and get paid by companies to discover exploits before the "bad guys" do.

Vulnerability

An exploit or problem within a program or network that can be used to gain extra access is referred to as a vulnerability. An exploit in the popular Sony video game console Playstation 3 let hackers install pirated games for free instead of paying for them. Finding an exploit or vulnerability is another large goal for hackers.

Bug

A glitch or problem within a program that produces unexpected results. Bugs can sometimes be used to make an exploit, so hackers are always checking for bugs in program, and security experts are always trying to resolve bugs.

Internet

The internet is a network of connected computers that can communicate with each other. Websites are available by communicating with web servers, and games can be played after connecting to a game server. Ultimately every computer on the internet can be communicated with by every other computer depending on the computer's security settings.

Intranet

By comparison, an INTRAnet is a local network consisting of only a few computers. Companies might use intranets to share files securely and without putting them through the entire internet where they could be intercepted. VPNs are usually used to connect to private intranets.

IP

An IP (Internet Protocol) address is the numerical identifier given to a device on a network. Every computer on the internet has a public IP, which is the IP that can geographically pinpoint a computer. We use IP addresses to connect to websites, but instead of typing a number such as 192.168.1.0, we type the domain name (google.com) which uses a DNS server to translate into the numerical IP.

You can learn your local/private IP address by typing *ipconfig* into a Windows command prompt. Some websites, such as http://whatismyipaddress.com/ can reveal your public IP address.

```
C:\windows\system32\cmd.exe

Windows IP Configuration

Ethernet adapter Local Area Connection:

   Connection-specific DNS Suffix  . :
   Link-local IPv6 Address . . . . . :
   IPv4 Address. . . . . . . . . . . : 10.1.15.33
   Subnet Mask . . . . . . . . . . . : 255.255.0.0
   Default Gateway . . . . . . . . . : 10.1.1.2
```

Chapter 4: Getting Started Hacking

Firstly, this book assumes that the aspiring hacker is using a Windows-based operating system. One of the best tools available on Windows is the command prompt, which can be accessed by following these directions:

1. Press and hold the windows button and the "r" key. This brings up "Run".

2. In the "Open:" field, type "cmd" and click okay.

3. The command prompt will open as a black terminal with white text.

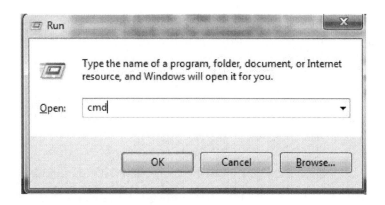

The command prompt resembles old DOS prompts or Linux terminals in aesthetics and functionality. Essentially, the entire computer can be interfaced through the command prompt without ever using a mouse, and this is how older computers worked! It is an essential tool for hackers because there are commands and hacking methods that are only possible through typing commands into the prompt.

C:\Users\name\>

is the current directory (folder) in which you are located. You can type "*dir*" and press enter to view the contents of the directory. To change folders, you would type "*cd foldername*". You can also go backwards by typing "*cd* ..". More commands can be viewed by typing "*help*". It is strongly encouraged that the aspiring hacker learn and master the command line, because cmd is a hacker's best friend!

Hacking is a broad term to describe a variety of methods to achieve an end goal of gaining access to a system. Although some hackers do it for fun, others do it for personal gain. No matter how it is achieved, it must come about through a variety of technical methods, which will be described below. A few might have a demonstration attached to them; feel free to start your hacking career by following along.

Social Engineering

Social engineering is a hacking technique that doesn't actually involve technical skill. In this method, an attacker gains access to information "socially".

Here is a story as an example. A clever hacker finds out that a certain employee of a company has a broken computer that they sent to IT to repair. The hacker calls the employee impersonating a new IT member and says that they are nearly finished with the repair, but they need her password to continue. If the disguise works, the employee will freely give over her password and the hacker is successful. Social engineering is extremely popular due to the trusting nature of people and cunning tricks that hackers have gained through experience.

Phishing

Phishing is a type of social engineering involving moderate technical skill. Derived from fishing, phishing is the act of "luring" employees to give information through email. Phishing can employ malware to accomplish its goal as well. Another story follows.

An accountant in the business office has finished payroll for the week, and they check their email to find an unread message. The subject: "URGENT: PAYROLL DECLINED" catches the accountant's attention. The email comes from payroll@adponline1.com, which the accountant has never seen before, but then again this problem has never happened previously so they do not know what to expect. "Your time clock readings did not come through correctly due to an authorization error. Please reply with your password for confirmation" reads the body. The clock reads 4:57, and everyone is about to go home, so the accountant is eager to get along with their day. Replying to the message with their password, the employee goes home, not realizing they just gave their password away to a hacker who now has access to payroll information.

Phishing is highly effective and usually the initial cause of data breaches. This fact comes about because of the general believability of phishing emails, which often use personal information to look legitimate. Additionally, most employees are not computer savvy enough to understand the difference between a fake password request and a real one.

Recently, many companies have begun allocating funds to security training programs for employees. These courses specifically teach how to guard against phishing attempts. Despite this, the brightest hackers will always be able to con and socially engineer their way into sensitive information.

DoS

Denial of Service (DoS) is an attack where multiple network requests are sent to a website or server in order to overload and crash it. DoS attacks can bring down infrastructure not prepared to handle large volumes of requests all at once. A few hackers use DoS attacks as a distraction or added nuisance to cover up their actual attack as it happens. Hackers can send individual network requests through the Windows command prompt as seen below:

Here, just a few bytes of data are being sent to google.com, but you can specify how many by altering the command like so:

ping –f –l 65500 websitename

The "*-f*" makes sure the packet is not fragmented or broken up, and "*-l*" lets you input a packet size from 32-65500, thereby increasing the size of the packet and the number of resources it consumes.

Now certainly the average hacker will never be able to take down a website such as google.com through ping requests on command prompt, so the above is for educational purposes only- real DoS attacks involve a powerful computer spamming the network with requests until the server slows to a crawl or crashes outright.

Anti-hackers respond to a high volume of traffic coming from a single origin by blocking that IP from making further requests. They can also observe the type of traffic flooding the server and block packet-types that look like DoS spam.

DDoS

Much more dangerous, DDoS (distributed denial of service) attacks are exponentially stronger than simple denial of service attacks. DDoS attacks involve attacking a server with multiple DoS attacks concurrently, each originating from various different locations. These attacks are much harder to block, because the original IP addresses are constantly changing, or there are just too many to block effectively.

One example of how devastating DDoS attacks can be came from the Sony attack of December 2014. Sony's newest game console (at the time) had just come out, and kids were opening them on Christmas day anxious to begin having fun. After hooking them up to the internet though, the disappointed kids were met with error messages stating that the Sony Network was down. The hacker collective Lizard Squad had been DDoSing Sony and overloading their game servers just for fun. Additionally, millions of new players were trying to access the service to play games and inquire about the down-time as well, which flooded the infrastructure even more. This created an issue for Sony, as they could not just block all requests because some were legitimate customers. The issue was finally resolved when the DDoSing was stopped, but the situation proved just how easily a coordinated network attack can cripple large servers.

Security Professionals have a few tools to prevent DDoS attacks from occurring. Load balancing hardware can spread out large requests among various servers, as to not bog down a single machine. They can also block the main sources of the attacks, pinging and DNS requests. Some companies, such as CloudFlare, offer web software that can actively identify and emergently block any traffic it believes is a DDoS attempt.

Performing DDoS attacks is relatively easy. Open-source software exists by the name of LOIC (Low Orbit Ion Cannon) that allows ease-of-use for DDoSing. The software can be seen below:

Rather humorous, the childish gui hides powerful tools that allow unskilled, beginner hackers to have DDoS capabilities when coordinating with others.

The most skilled attackers use botnets to increase their effectiveness. A well-written worm can infect data centers or universities with fast internet connections, and then these zombie computers all coordinate under the will of the hacker to attack a single target.

Fork Bomb

Fork bombs are a specific type of malicious code that works essentially like an offline DDoS. Instead of clogging network pipes, though, fork bombs clog processing pipes. Basically, a fork bomb is a process that runs itself recursively- that is the process copies itself over and over until the processor of a computer cannot keep up. If a hacker has access to a system and can run code, fork bombs are fairly deadly. Actually, fork bombs are one of the simplest programs to write. Typing "start" into a command prompt will open up another command prompt. This can be automated as demonstrated and pictured below.

1. Open notepad. (Windows+R, notepad, okay)

2. Type "start forkbomb.bat" as the first and only line.

3. Open the "save as" dialog.

4. Switch the file-type to "all files".

5. Name the file "forkbomb.bat", and then save the file.

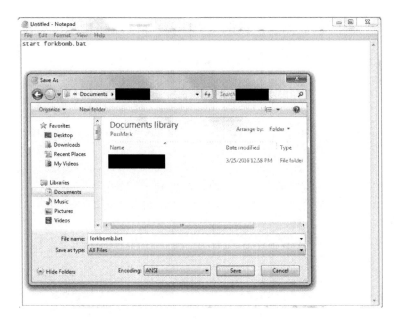

What we have just done is create a batch file in the same programming language that command prompt uses. Running this file (by right clicking its icon and then clicking "run") initiates the fork bomb, and it will continuously launch itself over and over until the computer cannot handle the resource strain. WARNING: Do not run this file unless you are prepared to face the consequences!

Cracking

Cracking is breaking into software/applications or passwords. Cracks can disable Digital Rights Management (DRM, also known as copy protection) on paid software so that full versions of software can be used without paying the full price. Skillful hackers achieve this by reverse-engineering code or finding exploits that let them run their own code. Encryption can be cracked as well, which leads to protected data being compromised since the attacker knows how to reverse the scrambling. Password cracking can be achieved through brute force cracking and dictionary attacks.

Brute Force

Brute force attacks attempt to guess a password by attempting *every* conceivable combination of letters and numbers. This was not terribly difficult in the days of DOS, where a password could only be 8 characters max. Brute force attacks are long and arduous, but can be successful on a powerful computer given enough time. Later in the chapter, we will talk about Kali Linux and its use as a security testing/hacking tool. Hydra is an application that can attempt to brute force passwords.

Dictionary Attack

Dictionary attacks are slightly more sophisticated. They are similar to brute force attacks in that they try a large combination of passwords, but they differ in the fact that dictionary attacks use a database of words from a dictionary to operate. This method works well at guessing passwords that are simple, such as one-word passwords. The application facilitating the dictionary attack will go through a large database of words starting at the top and try every one with slight variations to see if login is successful. The most clever dictionary attacks add words specific to the user to the database, such as their name, pets, work, birthday, etc... Most people use personal information as a password, and adding this information to a dictionary attack increases effectiveness.

Controlling a Colleague's Screen on Windows

Certain versions of Windows contain the "Remote Desktop" application built in, which is designed for IT personnel to quickly and remotely connect to a faraway computer to control and perform maintenance on it.

Remote desktop can be exploited (of course) and that is what we will do. This tutorial is designed for two computers on the same network, but clever users may be able to expand this to the entire internet.

Firstly, remote desktop needs to be enabled on both computers. Through control panel, click on "System" and then "Remote settings". Ensure "Allow Remote Assistance connections to this computer" is checked. Apply settings. Then, you will need your colleagues IP address; you may recall this can be done by typing *ipconfig* into a command prompt and copying the "IPv4 Address" listed.

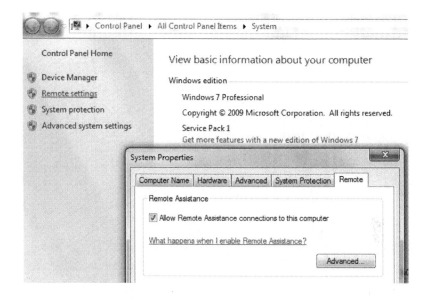

Now to initiate the remote control procedure, wait for the right time to surprise your friends and start the "Remote Desktop Connection" application on your computer (you can search for it in the start menu). Type in the friend's IP address and watch their surprised reaction when you move their mouse around!

Not technically a "hack", the remote desktop application CAN be used by hackers to spy on their targets. For example, an unsuspecting user may check bank account information while the hacker watches silently. This gives the hacker a good idea of passwords and personal information, so be wary if the remote desktop application is enabled on your computer.

Using another OS

Alternate operating systems are invaluable to a hacker for a variety of reasons. An easy way to try another operating system without overwriting the current one is to install the OS onto a bootable USB drive. We will demonstrate this process by installing Kali Linux (formally Backtrack Linux) onto a USB drive.

1. Download Kali Linux by visiting http://www.kali.org . You will need to download the version that is compatible with your processor (32 bit, 64 bit, or ARM). If in doubt, download the .iso file for 32 bit processors.

2. Download Rufus, the free USB writing software from http://rufus.akeo.ie

3. Plug in any USB storage stick with enough space for the Kali image. You might need 8GB or more depending on how big the image is at your time of reading.

4. WARNING: make sure the USB does not contain any valuable files- they will be deleted! Copy anything important off of the drive or you risk losing the data forever.

5. Start Rufus, select your USB stick from in the "Device" tab, and keep the rest of the settings default. Refer to the image below for the settings I have used.

6. Beside the checked "Create a bootable disk using" box, select "ISO Image" from the dropdown. Then click the box beside it and locate the Kali .iso.

7. Triple check that the information is correct, and that your USB has no important files still on it.

8. Click "Start".

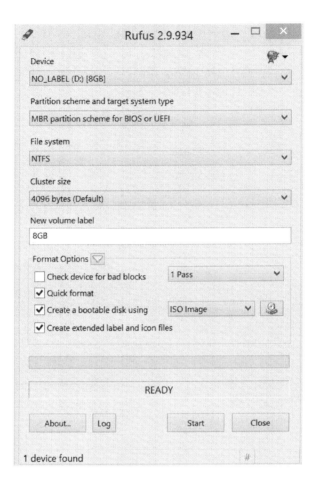

Rufus will take its time to finish. Once Rufus replies with "Done", it will have installed Kali Linux onto the USB and made it bootable. After finishing completely you are free to close out of the program.

For the next part of the process, you will need to shut your computer down completely. We need to access the BIOS of your computer. Continue reading on the next section and the process will continue.

BIOS/UEFI

The BIOS (Basic Input Output System) or UEFI (Unified Extensible Firmware Interface) of a computer is the piece of firmware that runs when the computer first powers on. Traditionally BIOS was used by default, but UEFI offers enhanced features and it is slowly replacing BIOS on computers. This startup firmware performs initialization, checks hardware, and provides options for the user to interact with their computer on the "bare metal" level. BIOS/UEFI interfaces can be accessed by pressing a key on the keyboard when the computer first starts up. The specific keyboard button needed varies between motherboard manufacturers, so the user needs to pay attention to their screen for the first few moments after powering on. After pressing the button, the computer will not boot into the operating system like normal, rather it will load the interface associated with BIOS/UEFI and give control to the user.

Continuing the demonstration of booting into an OS contained on a USB stick, the user now needs to set USB drives to boot before hard drives. Every motherboard manufacturer will use their own custom interface, so this book cannot explain the specific steps for each motherboard model. Basically, the goal is to find the "boot order", which is the order in which the computer checks for bootable operating systems. Under normal conditions, the computer will boot from the internal hard drive first, which is the probably the operating system you are reading this from now. We need to make sure the computer checks the USB drive for an OS before it checks internally. In the image below the hard drive is checked first, then the CD-ROM Drive is checked. Thirdly any removable devices are checked, but this specific computer would probably only get as far as the internal hard drive before finding the primary OS and booting. To boot into our image on the USB drive, move "Removable Devices" to the top of the list. Finally, ensure that the USB is plugged in, save changes to BIOS/UEFI, and reboot. The computer should begin loading Kali Linux.

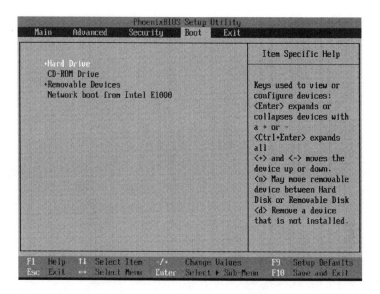

Any problems with booting will give an error message that the user can internet search to troubleshoot, but more than likely the computer will boot into Kali successfully. The user can now use a whole new operating system!

Kali Linux was chosen because of the tools that are available to it by default. Kali is often the go-to OS for hackers due to the software included. Hackers and security professionals alike chose Kali, so it is encouraged that aspiring minds experiment with the OS.

Using another OS to steal data

Here is an interesting point: through the bootable Kali USB you can also load your primary internal hard drive and view the contents. This means that you can access the files on your disk *without booting into Windows*. Try opening up your internal hard drive and viewing your personal files. Sometimes it is shocking to realize how easy it is to view personal data without really turning on Windows. Now admittedly there are a few restrictions on accessing protected data, but this technique can be used to recover secret information from a computer that does not belong to a hacker. Remember, if a computer is accessible physically, hackers have a significant advantage. They could always load up their favorite bootable OS, copy all data in the hard drive, and leave without ever logging into Windows. Even password protected or encrypted data is vulnerable to be copied. Since the attacker has a copy of the locked data, they can spend unlimited time trying to crack the password.

We will take a look at some of the other hacking tools present in Kali Linux below.

Port Scanning

Hacking is made easier with knowledge of the target infrastructure. One of the best ways to map out networks is through port scanning. Scanning ports reveals open points in a network. Having certain ports open can offer unique exploits for hackers, so hackers usually port scan prior to deciding a point-of-entry. On Kali Linux the best tool to do this is nmap. By loading Kali Linux onto a networked computer and running a terminal (Linux version of command prompt, open with ctrl+alt+T), the hacker can enter this command to scan a computer for open ports:

nmap -sV IPADDRESS -A –v

The terminal will run the nmap program with the specified parameters and begin scanning the specified IP address for open ports.

Packet Capture

Traffic through the network is sent as little pieces of data called packets. Each packet contains various bits, such as where it is coming from, where it is going, and whatever information is being sent. An unsecure network might be sending important information as plain, unencrypted text. Data sent this way is open for interception, and that is done through packet capture. Kali Linux has a built in application that does this- Wireshark. Wireshark is also available on Windows, for those that haven't seen the benefits of Kali. Packet capture is done by starting the application, changing your network card's mode to "promiscuous", and starting the packet capture.

Knowledgeable hackers can then view the packets that are captured and study them for information. Plain text will be visible if it is being sent that way, but encrypted text will be obscured.

SQL injection

SQL is a programming language mostly used on web servers; an example of typical code is below. SQL injections exploit poor coding on a website's login script through a clever "injection" of hacker-written code. This is a difficult process to explain, but it can be viewed through YouTube videos and website demos (http://www.codebashing.com/sql_demo).

```
drop table t1
Create table t1 (tim int, rem varchar(100))
select 86400
INSERT INTO t1 VALUES (1251781074, 'day1')
INSERT INTO t1 VALUES (1251781074 + 86400, 'day2')
INSERT INTO t1 VALUES (1251781074 + 2*86400, 'day3')
INSERT INTO t1 VALUES (1251781074 + 3*86400, 'day4')
INSERT INTO t1 VALUES (1251781074 + 4*86400, 'day5')

Select DATEADD(hour,-4,(dateadd(second ,tim, '1/1/1970'))), * From t1

DECLARE @StartDateTime DATETIME
,@EndDateTime DATETIME

SELECT @StartDateTime = '2009-09-02 00:57:54.000'
SELECT @EndDateTime = '2009-09-03 00:57:54.000 '

Select * from t1
where
 DATEADD(hour,-4,(dateadd(second ,tim, '1/1/1970'))) >= @StartDateTime
AND DATEADD(hour,-4,(dateadd(second ,tim, '1/1/1970'))) <= @EndDateTime
```

Destroying a Linux-based System

Linux-based operating systems are generally more secure than their Windows counterparts, but the design philosophy behind UNIX-like kernels is that superusers (administrators) have total control with no questions asked. Windows administrators generally have full control as well, but the operating system prevents the user from accidentally damaging their system! One very malicious attack involves exploiting the superuser's permissions to delete the entire Linux operating system.

While experimenting with the terminal in Kali Linux, you might have noticed that some commands require "sudo" as a preface. Sudo invokes superuser permissions and allows system-changing commands to run after the root password is input. Since the Linux kernel gives full controls to superusers, entering the following command will completely delete the operating system *even while it is running*.

sudo rm −rf /

Under no circumstance should this command ever be run without permission. This command will break the operating system! Even when testing this command on yourself, be prepared to face the consequences. You cannot blame this guide if something goes wrong. The anatomy of the command is as follows:

Sudo invokes superuser and gives complete control, *rm* signifies remove, *-rf* tells *rm* to remove nested folders and files, and / starts the deletion process at the very first folder. Thusly the entire system is deleted. If the computer doesn't immediately crash, it certainly will not boot after a shutdown.

Chapter 5: Building Skill and Protecting Oneself

Programming

Learning to code is what separates "script kiddies" from actual elite hackers. Any aspiring hacker should take the time and learn the basics of programming in a variety of languages. A good beginner language is the classic C++. Based on original C, C++ is basic high-level programming language that is powerful and easy enough for first time learners. A variety of books exist on learning the language, and it is recommended for novices.

Programming is an essential skill because most exploits involve using programming code to alter or bypass a system. Viruses and other malware are written with code also, and competent hacker-coders can write awe-inspiring applications such as ransomware.

Mastering Terminal and Command Prompt

Ultimately the terminal is an application that can parse programming code one line at a time. Skillful hackers have mastered moving around the command prompt and terminal. As previously stated, typing *help* into command prompt provides a list of commands. In Linux's bash terminal a user can type *man* (for manual) to learn about commands. Manual pages are long and extremely detailed.

Routers and WEP

Understanding what password protection is used for a Wi-Fi router/access point could potentially help a hacker crack the password. In the early days of Wi-Fi, WEP was used for password security. WEP is an algorithm that lacked complexity and was replaced by WPA in 2004. However, many routers still use WEP by accident or default. This gives hackers a common exploit, because WEP keys are crackable in a short amount of time. To do this on Kali Linux a hacker must start the OS on a laptop with wireless within range of the WEP access point. Then, they would open a terminal and use the airmon-ng application.

Cracking WPA keys is much more time consuming due to the increased complexity, but WEP keys are easy targets for hackers to practice their emerging skills.

Protecting Oneself as a Hacker

Curious hackers that are learning skills mentioned in this book must take care to protect themselves. Any serious infiltration attempt should only be attempted on a network in which the individual has permission to experiment and penetration test. Depending on the state or federal laws of the reader, various police action could be taken against an individual without explicit permission to perform this book's demonstrations; astute hackers would already be wary of this.

All of this aside, it is beneficial for aspiring hackers to learn various methods to keep themselves safe from identification. Additionally, many hacktivists attempting to reveal the illegal activities of the company (whistleblowing) in which they work are monitored constantly. Only through some of the subjects we talk about below are these people safe from the oppressive nature that employers can inflict. General security is not only a decent practice, security can protect those trying to protect others. For hackers, security safeguards against "counter-hacks" and keeps the field advancing.

Password Security

The largest difference between the average computer user and a security expert would be password complexity. While the average employee might use "fido82" for their authentication key, security experts might use something less guessable such as "Fsdf3@3". Sharp hackers will take advantage of this fact when dictionary attacking passwords. Furthermore, some passwords and infrastructures will be too well-protected for any beginner to break. As skill increases, hackers become wiser. Sage-like hackers can produce new exploits seemingly out of thin-air, and it is assured that any person can achieve this level with enough practice.

With self-introspection, attackers and hactivists alike must live up to the standards that security experts live by. A strong personal password will nearly guarantee that a hacker cannot be "counter-hacked". As we will read in the next few sections, most hackers are persecuted because their devices are seized and easily counter-hacked to reveal nefarious activity. Complex passwords will stand up to the robust supercomputers of federal governments.

It is also recommended to never write passwords down or save them to a file somewhere. The best passwords are random, memorized, and secret.

Password Leaks

Furthermore, security experts will rarely repeat passwords. Shockingly, plenty of users do just that- the average person uses the same password for banking, social media, forums, and online shopping! 2015's Ashley Madison leak saw the online publication of email addresses; 2013's Tumblr leak had passwords going up for sale on the "darknet" (black market internet). Since users rarely change passwords, savvy hackers can search these databases and locate user information. The passwords have most likely stayed the same, so the hacker has effortlessly gained access to an account. Password leaks are common and readily searchable on the internet too, just access https://haveibeenpwned.com/ to check if a password is compromised! Conclusively, these leaks do not hurt users that change passwords regularly and keep them different for each account.

Encryption

Encryption is available to Windows users that are on a Professional/Enterprise version by default. Otherwise, a user wishing to encrypt files will have to download a 3rd party application such as TrueCrypt (http://www.truecrypt.org). Encryption is essential for users wishing to protect any kind of data. Whether it is bad poetry, trade secrets, or a log of successful hacks, the files need to be encrypted if you want to guarantee that absolutely nobody should be able to read it. Snoopy roommates will therefore not be able to access the contents of the file without your expressed permission, and law enforcement officials that seize a computer reach a dead end when greeted with the prompt for a decryption password.

The process is done on Windows by right clicking a file, accessing the properties, clicking the advanced properties button in the "Attributes" section, then checking the "Encrypt contents to secure data" checkbox. A screenshot is visible below:

Every tip previously offered about passwords applies when choosing a decryption key. It is essential to remember that if a beginner hacker could break the encryption, then certainly the combined intelligence power of a government could crack the key as well.

History

Although obvious, not many novices realize that computer history can compromise an operation. For the uninitiated, browser history is a log of visited websites that is stored on a computer. This list if often not encrypted, so a compromised list with "how to hack" on recent searches could be incriminating evidence when brought before a court. Most computer users disable browser history altogether for privacy reasons, and the process is not difficult. In Firefox, for example, the option is found under the "Privacy" tab of "Options". Disabling history is useful, but clearing out previous history might be needed as well. Once again the methodology varies, but the general process is to access the list of recently viewed websites and clear it through a button or command.

History is not always exclusively stored locally. Some ISPs (Internet Service Providers, the organizations that provide users with internet access) keep their own log of internet history. Police subpoenas would require them to hand over this history, which basically voids the care put into deleting internet history. There are ways around this fact however, which will be explicated in the following sections.

Using a Proxy

The reason that ISPs know internet history is related to how hackers intercept packets to view information. Regular, unencrypted webpage traffic is predicable in how it looks and can therefore be captured. Internet service providers sometimes keep this information by habit or law, so the only way to remove this annoyance is to disguise the data packets as something else entirely. Proxies allow users to do this. Normal packets will have the source and destination address clearly marked, while a packet sent through a proxy will not show the initial sender, only the proxy machine that relayed the packets. On the ISP's end, it seems as though the computer is communicating with one address while they are really communicating with another. When a court subpoenas the ISP for information, there is no link between the source (hacker) and the ultimate destination (target).

Proxies can be used through a web browser (hide.me, whoer.net, proxysite.com, etc...) or as a 3rd party piece of software. Proxies are most famously used in college networks to evade content filtering-nobody can block your gaming websites if it looks like you are connecting to something else entirely.

Proxies do have their downsides, though. Law agencies with enough power can retrieve records from a proxy server and match up "timestamps" of your connections to piece together your internet history. Using multiple proxies only delays the inevitable, because if detectives have one proxy server compromised then they can just keep tracing them from proxy to proxy until the origin address is reached.

Using a VPN

Earlier in the book VPNs were explained to "tunnel" data through a network. This service is usually used by employees to work from home, but hackers can exploit VPNs to work as an enhanced proxy of sorts. A typical VPN alters packets in such a way as to encrypt them and make them unreadable. The packets will not look like web activity, because they are sent through a different port entirely. This adds a layer of complexity to the packets that suits their use for security. For example, a public, open network is dangerous to check your bank statements on, because the packets can be readily intercepted and decoded by hackers. Using a VPN, though, hides the data and allows normal, unrestricted use that is not in danger of being decrypted.

Competent hackers will use the proxy-like qualities of a VPN to hide their true location. Usually these servers are moderately more secure from government agencies as well due to the added obscurity and difficulty of determining origin points. Internet pirates are quite fond of virtual private networks because they can conceal the illegal data they download as regular, protected data.

VPNs are usually created through 3rd party software. The program OpenVPN allows anybody to connect to a VPN server, but they will most likely need a username and password. Organizations typically have private VPNs that act as relays only to company intranets, and these relays need company provided passwords. Individuals that wish to use a VPN might have to pay money for the ability to connect to a VPN server, but hackers agree VPNs are money well spent.

Tor Project

For hackers and security experts seeking the highest level of protection, the Tor Project (http://torproject.org) offers a solution. The company offers a piece of free software called Tor, which acts as a super-VPN/proxy. Tor bounces internet traffic across thousands of relays (each with substantial encryption) to ensure that the destination and origin of the packets are not clear. This software can be used by any individual wishing to hide their online activities, and it has proved decently effective.

Browser Fingerprint

Somewhat of an advanced topic, browser fingerprinting is an elaborate anti-hacking technique where specific unique information contained in your web browser (language packs, ad-ons, OS version, etc...) is retained by websites and used to identify users. Most hackers use unique configurations with adblocking plugins, IP obscuring software, and other defining characteristics. The irony of this is that the uniqueness gained from protecting oneself becomes an identifying factor through device fingerprinting.

Basically, the best way to stay hidden on the internet is to "blend in" with the crowd, so a unique configuration cannot be traced back to a hacker. Since this is such an advanced and emerging topic, it is too early to say whether detectives and cyber investigators are catching criminals with this methodology. A browser fingerprint can be viewed through online testers, such as https://amiunique.org.

Open Source vs. Proprietary

Throughout this book some software has been referred to as "free". The actual correct term for the software is FOSS (free and open source software). Programs that are FOSS are not only monetarily free, they are also transparent in their coding. Open-source refers to the fact that the coding of the program is visible at any time, whereas proprietary software's code is not visible ever. This fact is important; if code is not visible, there is no way to know exactly what the program is doing or who it is sending data to. Proprietary software, such as Google's web browser Chrome, unquestionably sends data back to Google. Contrasting starkly is Mozilla's FOSS Firefox web browser. Firefox has transparent code, so at any time programmers can read through the source and know for certain whether Firefox sends data back.

Hackers and security-minded people tend to gravitate towards FOSS because of its more safe nature. After all, nobody knows exactly what is going on under the hood of some dubious proprietary programs. There might exist backdoors for governments that would expose good-natured hackers or whistleblowers within closed-source software, so the best security is always done through well maintained free and open source software.

Throwaways

Whistleblowers and other high level leakers (see: Edward Snowden) require the utmost privacy with zero chance of linking an action to a person. Many professionals decide to do their private doings through throwaway devices.

A throwaway is a computer that is only used for the private doings. It is usually bought with cash, has no mention of the buyer's name, is never used to log into accounts associated with the buyer, and is used in a public place such as a coffee shop. If used correctly, there should not be a single shred of evidence pointing back to the buyer.

It is important that throwaways be bought with cash because a bill of sale with a name on it is an undeniable link. It is for these reasons that hackers rarely, if ever, use credit cards for purchases. Cash is virtually untraceable, but security cameras can still pick out a face in a store. Buying used or from yard sales removes any monitoring capabilities an organization might have had.

Signing into personal accounts leaves traces on the device, and using personal internet connections will lead back to the IP registered to you by the ISP. Coffee Shops, McDonalds, libraries, and internet cafes usually offer free internet without signing up- these places are the locations of choice for anonymity.

Bitcoin

If something must be bought online, bitcoin is an anonymous way to do so. Bitcoin is a virtual currency that isn't attached to a name. Criminals in the past have used bitcoin to purchase illegal substances on the "darknet", which proves how anonymous bitcoin can be.

Conclusion

The demonstrations in this book are admittedly basic, for they were provided to stimulate an interest in security/hacking. Hackers must cultivate their skill through practice and studying. To gain skill, you must study networking basics, security concepts, programming languages, cryptography, and much more. Endurance and tenacity mold the brightest into outstanding hackers, so lifelong learning should be an aspiration for any hacker. Your journey continues with great hope and promise.

Thank you again for downloading this book!

I hope this book was able to help you to understand some of the core concepts revolving around security, hacking, and counter-hacking. The scope of the subject is so large that this book could not ever hope to cover everything. Even though the time spent on various subjects in this book was brief, I encourage you to research them further.

Remember that security and hacking are relevant today more than ever. This book encourages curious minds to inspire to adhere to the "hacker's manifesto" and be guilty of no crime save curiosity. This book does not encourage illegal activity, it encourages exploration and entertainment.

Finally, if you enjoyed this book, please take the time to share your thoughts and post a review on Amazon. It'd be greatly appreciated!

Thank you and good luck!

Made in the USA
Middletown, DE
04 October 2016